Christopher Wright

GEORGES DE LA TOUR

PHAIDON

The author and publishers would like to thank all those museum authorities and private owners who have kindly allowed works in their possession to be reproduced.

Phaidon Press Limited, Littlegate House, St Ebbe's Street, Oxford
Published in the United States of America by E. P. Dutton, New York

First published 1977

© *1977 by Phaidon Press Limited*

ISBN 0 7148 1807 0

Library of Congress Catalog Card Number: 77-75402

Printed in Great Britain

GEORGES DE LA TOUR

Less than forty paintings survive from the hand of Georges de La Tour and they are widely scattered in the museums and private collections of Western Europe and America. A few of these pictures count amongst the most sensitive candlelight pictures ever painted. La Tour's fame as one of the most individual painters of his time, ranking with Vermeer of Delft, is very recent indeed. It dates back to 1972, when almost all his surviving pictures were brought together for a memorable exhibition held in Paris at the Orangerie des Tuileries.

The story of the rediscovery of La Tour after more than two centuries of complete oblivion is worth repeating as an interesting illustration of how a great painter can gradually return to favour by quite unexpected means. Indeed a question frequently asked is: how could a painter of La Tour's quality be neglected for so long?

La Tour died in 1652 in Lunéville in the Duchy of Lorraine, formerly German, but annexed by France in the 1630s. La Tour's death was recorded in the parish registers of the town. His name appears but rarely, and then only with a passing mention, in the numerous histories of the Duchy written in the eighteenth and nineteenth centuries. It was not until 1863 that the archivist of the town of Lunéville, Alexandre Joly, discovered and published a series of the municipal account books dating from the years 1644–52. These account books recorded a number of quite large payments to a painter of the town – Georges de La Tour – for pictures commissioned by the town authorities. They were intended as annual New Year gifts to the Maréchal de La Ferté, the French Governor of Nancy. Unfortunately Joly was not able to find any pictures by this mysterious painter who had obviously been highly esteemed in his time. There were no pictures in Lunéville which could possibly correspond to the descriptions in the documents – a *St. Alexis*, a *St. Sebastian*, a *Nativity* and a *Denial of Peter*. In fact at that time only two pictures bearing La Tour's signature were known at all; both of them were on the other side of France, in the Museum at Nantes and both were wrongly attributed in spite of the signatures.

Joly's article was laid to rest in that special category of obscurity reserved for provincial erudition. The next step, in 1899, was the publication, again locally in a limited edition, of the registers of all the births, marriages and deaths in the town of Lunéville from the middle of the sixteenth century onwards. In the register were listed the baptisms of all La Tour's children except one, and his own and his wife's death. Again this passed unnoticed. A year later, L. Gonse – in one of those once fashionable books on the treasures of French provincial museums – remarked 'in spite of himself', that two pictures he had seen – one at Epinal thought to represent the Angel visiting St. Peter in prison, the other the *Newborn Child* at Rennes – were possibly by the same hand. Neither picture was signed; the Epinal picture was identified as *Job Mocked by his Wife* in the 1930s, and the La Tour signature was discovered only in 1972 during cleaning.

Gonse's comparison was not followed up by any other writer. The first positive step towards the reconstruction of La Tour's work was taken in 1915 by a German scholar, Hermann Voss, in a short-lived periodical whose circulation in war-torn Europe was understandably limited to Germany. Voss attributed five pictures to La Tour, including the Rennes *Newborn Child*, and the *Dream of Joseph* and the *Denial of Peter* both at Nantes and both signed. Probably unaware of Gonse's comment, Voss did not include the Epinal *Job Mocked by his Wife*.

The number of pictures thought to be by La Tour's hand had risen to nine by 1934, when they were all brought together in Paris for the exhibition *Les Peintres de La Réalité*. This sudden presentation to the French public of a totally unknown painter gave an impetus to researchers which culminated in the monumental work of François-Georges Pariset, published in 1948. By that time most of the documents had been collated and published, including the place and year of the artist's birth. Since that time very few new documents of importance have been found; but new pictures have continued to be discovered, especially in the 1960s and early 1970s. These discoveries revealed the true depth of La Tour's genius. For instance the *The Dice Platers*, discovered in 1972, showed that La Tour's candlelight scenes were not all devoted to religious subjects. This discovery was followed immediately by another – *The Payment of Dues*, also a secular subject and also a candlelight, which was identified in the Museum of Lvov.

The few facts about La Tour's life as they are now known can be summarized as follows. He was born in 1593 the son of a baker at Vic-sur-Seille, a small town which was under the jurisdiction of the Bishop of Metz. By 1617 he was already recorded as a painter in Vic at the time of his marriage to the wealthy Diane Le Nerf, whose family lived at nearby Lunéville in the Duchy of Lorraine. In 1620 La Tour moved to his wife's home town where he remained resident for the rest of his life.

Apart from his signature on legal documents, only two specimens of La Tour's handwriting survive. One of them – a petition to the Duke of Lorraine asking him for exemption from taxes in his new home in Lunéville – is especially revealing: La Tour states that he wished to move to Lunéville because there were no other painters active either in or near the town. Thus, on his own admission he worked in almost total artistic isolation. According to the documents, only one other painter seems to have been active locally – an obscure artist of Swiss origin, Claude Dogoz, who worked in Vic. No work from his hand is known to survive.

La Tour's artistic education is a matter for speculation. It is probable that he was largely self-taught as a young man, but became receptive to the influence of other artists as he grew older. After his arrival in Lunéville in 1620 at the age of twenty-seven, there are not sufficient gaps in the documents to allow of a prolonged educational sojurn abroad. Rome, Utrecht and Paris have been suggested by different scholars as places he may have visited. His style offers no clues: it remained his own. Towards the end of his life, however, it is possible to detect outside influences in his art, especially from such painters as Honthorst and Gerard Seghers.

The Lunéville years (1620–1652) are documented in the sense that the records show La Tour to have engaged in financial transactions and the acquisition of property, but his artistic career is still largely a matter of surmise. He certainly set up a studio and employed apprentices, one by one, on rather strict terms. He appears to have been relatively prosperous, since he acquired property. But apart from the two small pictures acquired by the Duke of Lorraine in 1623 and 1624, there is no record of a painting being bought until 1644, by which time La Tour was already fifty-one.

La Tour's character, however, is rather less a matter for speculation. By twentieth-century standards he seems to have been bad-tempered and unpleasant. He was fined for leaving rubbish in front of his house. He extracted money mercilessly from those in debt to

4

him, and he is known to have hit one unfortunate inhabitant of Lunéville so hard that the town authorities had to call in a doctor. Finally, in 1646, the exasperated inhabitants of the town were driven to write a petition to the administration at Nancy listing La Tour's crimes. He was especially unpopular because he kept a large number of dogs which trampled down the corn. Some of La Tour's best pictures are so perfect, calm, orderly and elevated in spirit that it is difficult to imagine that they were produced by such an odious human being.

How could it be that a painter isolated from his contemporaries could arrive at such a high point of achievement, epitomized by the Rennes *Newborn Child* (Plates 40 and 41)?

There have been many attempts to chart his development towards the *Newborn Child* but even the most persuasive result is not entirely convincing. There are many problems posed by the early group of pictures and each new scrap of evidence only serves to confuse the problem still further.

The usual method employed by historians in reconstructing an artist's career involves a knowledge of his patrons. In La Tour's instance they appear to have been few in number. Apart from the Duke of Lorraine, the town of Lunéville (at least from 1644 onwards) also acted as his patron. The other *probable* important connection was Louis XIII of France. The only evidence for this is the fact that La Tour described himself, when acting as godfather at a christening at Nancy in 1639, as '*peintre ordinaire du roi*'. No contemporary reference has been found recording contact with the French King, but a hundred years later Dom Calmet, when writing a history of Lorraine, recorded a story to the effect that Louis XIII had had in his bedroom a *St. Sebastian* by La Tour, which he admired so much that he ordered all pictures by other artists to be removed from the room. Dom Calmet added that La Tour had also painted a similar picture for the Duke of Lorraine.

The next line of research involves the artistic background of Nancy, the capital of the Duchy, in the first thirty years of the century. What is known is scant indeed, but a few clues are offered as to the type of artistic environment La Tour would have observed from a distance during his youth.

The most important picture to arrive in those years was a large *Annunciation* by Caravaggio or an immediate follower, which was in Nancy as early as 1616. If modern scholarship is right in the way it has reconstructed La Tour's early artistic career (Plates 1–17), it is clear that this monumental and heavily shadowed work, which is still at Nancy in the Musée des Beaux-Arts, had little effect on the young La Tour directly. But Caravaggio may have had an indirect stylistic effect. The court painter Jacques Bellange (died after 1617), used the Caravaggio *Annunciation* as the basis for his own etching of the subject. Bellange also made etchings of beggars brawling and a standing hurdy-gurdy player, and it was images of this type, rather than those of Caravaggio himself, which supplied the sources for La Tour's early pictures.

The group of pictures thought to be from the hand of the young La Tour show a disconcerting difference from his mature art, not only in the handling of the paint but also in his approach to the subject. This early group is quite homogeneous in style. None of them is signed, dated or documented and none can be traced back earlier than the late eighteenth century.

One of the most striking and beautifully painted is a pair, the *Peasant* (Plate 2) and the *Peasant's Wife* (Plates 1 and 3). From their poses, it seems that the woman is remonstrating with her husband and this has led to the reasonable assumption that they are both fragments of one much larger picture. It may have been a scene from a play; but as there are no other surviving pictures of this type from Lorraine this has to remain speculation.

Very similar in technique but rather coarser is the *Vegetable Eaters* (Plate 4). At the time of their discovery in 1975, the two figures were in fact separated but they have now been joined together again to make one composition. Pictures of this type, with its total lack of compassion for the unpleasant sight of a poor old couple eating their meagre ration, pose the question of how La Tour could have eventually arrived at the carefully distilled style epitomized by the *Dream of Joseph* and the *Newborn Child*. The only parallel that springs to mind is the astonishing difference between the young Velazquez in his *Water-Seller of Seville* (London, Wellington Museum) and the mature artist in his celebrated *Rokeby Venus* (London, National Gallery). But Velazquez is not as enigmatic as La Tour; his work can be seen to develop quite logically from one extreme to the other. There are no satisfactory intermediary pictures for La Tour.

In a similar vein to the *Vegetable Eaters* is the *Beggars' Brawl* (Plate 5), which is an equally unsympathetic record of low life. La Tour is almost mocking; there is no dignity in the struggle of the blind old man, only the heartless mockery of his fellows.

The two compositions of the *Hurdy-Gurdy Player* are slightly more refined. The version with the dog (Plate 8), although much damaged, reveals a certain sympathy in the painting of the bright-eyed little dog at the old man's feet. But the old man's face with its scar is reminiscent of the misery of the *Beggars' Brawl* and the *Vegetable Eaters*. The other *Hurdy-Gurdy Player* (Plate 9), unlike all the other pictures in this group, has been known for a long time – ever since it was acquired by the Nantes Museum in 1810.

Both pictures are strikingly realistic, as befits subjects that must have been a common sight in La Tour's time (they frequently appear in Dutch art.) La Tour's images are life-size, increasing the impression of reality. So brilliant is the technique that the spectator can almost hear the cacophony created by the noisy instruments and the wheezy voices of the old men. The pictures are painted with consummate skill, which finds its most unexpected expression, in the large blue-bottle resting by the hurdy-gurdy (detail, Plate 10) – a device perhaps intended as a miniature *tour de force*, perhaps as a means of heightening the feeling of squalor. As with so much in La Tour's work, one can only guess at the purpose.

All the subjects mentioned so far have been secular, but running parallel to them is another group of stylistically related religious pictures. The two saints, *St. Judas Thaddeus* (Plate 6) and *St. James the Less* (Plate 7), form part of a set of which the rest are copies. It is likely that the small *Image St. Pierre* acquired by the Duke of Lorraine in 1624 was of this type. The saints are rugged, almost violent, as if they are characters out of the *Beggars' Brawl* with the symbols of martyrdom added.

Two other religious pictures, the *St. Jeromes* (Plates 12 and 13), are similar in colour and in handling. The more dramatic of the two is the Grenoble version: the rope the saint has used to flagellate himself is discoloured with his blood. It is almost as if the painter is pushing further and further towards an extreme, an extreme of understated violence. His desolate figures are put in an unreal world of empty space inhabited only by indeterminate shadows and odd stones.

Nobody knows why or when La Tour suddenly produced three pictures which are quite unlike anything else he had done so far. Much discussion has taken place as to their dating but it seems unlikely that the artist who created the very special world of the *Cheat* and the

Fortune Teller (Plate 15) would have gone on to paint the *Beggars' Brawl*. In the *Cheat* (which exists in two versions, compared in detail in Plates 16 and 17) La Tour creates an unexpected atmosphere of a courtesan and her assistants duping a little rich boy. Stylistic connections between the *Cheat* and the earlier group of pictures are hard to find, but there is a certain similarity, for instance, in the folds of the dress on the youth on the right of *The Cheat* and the cloak of the *Hurdy-Gurdy Player*.

But it is the mentality of the two *Cheats* and the *Fortune Teller* which provides the surprise. It is a world of sideways glances, of prostitution, of blatant cheating. The ultimate source for this type of picture is Caravaggio himself who painted both a *Cheat* (now lost) and a *Fortune Teller* (Paris, Musée du Louvre). Caravaggio must have painted both these pictures in the late 1590s when he preferred a very bland palette without dramatic lighting effects. Their influence certainly percolated through to La Tour, but how he came so close to his source remain a mystery.

Such an uncanny derivation from Caravaggio himself has led many writers to speculate on the extent to which the mature La Tour may have travelled. The only piece of circumstantial evidence for his having *painted* outside Lunéville after his arrival there in 1620 is his signature on the *Fortune Teller*:'Luneuilla Lothar'. If it is genuine – and there have been doubts about the unusual calligraphy – the words imply that the picture was painted outside Lorraine, for it was the custom for painters in the seventeenth century to place the town or country of origin on their pictures when they were abroad.

The *Fortune Teller,* impressive though it is as a composition, has presented a number of problems for La Tour scholars. In colour it is very close to the Geneva *Cheat* and it is almost as if they were intended as a pair. The *Fortune Teller* has been cut at the right and extended at the top. The impossible perspective of the figure on the extreme left could well have been caused by some repainting at a later date.

The pictures so far discussed fall into two quite distinct groups. There is no satisfactory means of dating them. Only the Louvre *Cheat* and the *Fortune Teller* are signed. Even when we have some evidence it proves to be tantalizingly inconclusive. It is for instance clear that the figure on the right of the *Beggars' Brawl* is derived from an engraving after the Dutch artist Hendrick Terbrugghen. The Terbrugghen painting from which the engraving was probably derived is dated 1627. But we know that Terbrugghen repeated the same composition throughout his career in the 1620s in Utrecht and therefore it is not safe to say that the *Beggars' Brawl* is after 1627.

All these pictures are very distant indeed from the world of La Tour's maturity. In order to achieve the miracle of the *Newborn Child* La Tour must have experimented with night effects. In fact a few pictures that may be from his hand show evidence of this. In the *St. Jerome Reading* (Plate 19), which is tragically damaged, especially in the face, there is a wonderfully subtle effect of the light shining through the paper he is reading. The *St. Jerome Reading* is not so far from the equally damaged *St. Philip* (Plate 18) which is itself an original from the series of *Saints* of which two originals survive at Albi (Plates 6 and 7). But *St. Jerome Reading* offers no real indication of what is to come. There is no hint of the radical change that led La Tour to remove completely from his art all suggestion of violence and replace it with a monumental calm. It could well be that the *Payment of Dues* (Plate 20) is one of the first night scenes, but the reading of the date is still uncertain. Even the subject of this recently discovered picture has not been satisfactorily explained. Apart from this picture, which is still restless in its composition, La Tour's mature style is remarkably consistent. But the order in which these pictures were painted is not clear. It is likely that La Tour repeated himself from time to time, producing similar versions of the same composition. There are two almost identical versions of the *Magdalen with the Night-Light* (one is shown on Plates 26 and 27; the other is in a private collection). Also he made several variations on the same theme. Thus there are three quite different versions on the theme of the penitent Magdalen (a second is shown on Plates 28 and 29).

There is still considerable disagreement as to which pictures represent the artist's first mature work. The two most favoured – but by no means unanimously accepted – candidates are *The Flea Catcher* and *Job Mocked by his Wife*. Costume experts have noted that the very high waist of the dress which Job's wife is wearing did not become fashionable until the 1630s; and the two pictures are sufficiently similar in style to suppose that they were painted at approximately the same time.

Certainly *The Flea Catcher* leads quite logically into the *Penitent Magdalen* group. It is one of La Tour's most subtle and monumental compositions. Its real meaning has never been satisfactorily explained. The flea-catcher may be crushing a flea between her fingernails; or she may have just seized it in the folds of her robe. Does the candle on the chair have any significance? Is the woman pregnant? La Tour refuses to reveal the secret of this lonely figure in a bare room.

The technique of this and the other related pictures is unique and subtle. Working in isolation, he painted in a very personal way. He often used a very thin, transparent brownish ground over which he laid, equally thinly, the darker shadows, keeping the whole very simple. The half-tones were then added equally simply, almost to the point of abbreviation of the forms. Then the lighted areas were painted with consummate skill. He used all the various techniques which oil painting permitted: impasto, scumbling, glazing. All these characteristics are visible in *The Flea Catcher* where they are in perfect harmony. The red chair-back is a simple area of tone, as are the furniture legs. The woman's hands, lit by the glare of the candle and shown in detail, contrast with the softly-lit face.

Many of these characteristics appear to a greater or lesser extent in La Tour's other mature pictures. In the *Newborn Child* the impasto is played down and replaced by a kind of pointillism. In *Job Mocked by his Wife* great sweeps of the brush loaded with blood-coloured paint are used to define the shadowy folds of the woman's gown. But the rest of the picture is very similar in handling to *The Flea Catcher*. From the point of view of human drama it is one of La Tour's most touching compositions. Job's wife is depicted as a termagent and Job himself is seen as a pathetic old man helpless against his wife's unthinking tirade. Yet La Tour also detaches himself from the drama and goes on to paint the points of light on Job's knuckles with the objectivity used for a candle flame or a chairback.

In the Magdalen series, the candle appears but it plays a rather different rôle from the explicit one in *Job* and *The Flea Catcher*. The *Penitent Magdalen* in the Wrightsman collection (not reproduced here for technical reasons) is unusual in La Tour's work because it shows the candle flame reflected in an elaborate mirror. The Washington *Magdalen* (Plate 28) is a grave picture. Colour has been drained from it. (La Tour also used this technique when he painted his interpretation of religious ecstasy, the *St. Francis* at Le Mans.) The Magdalen has rejected all her worldly luxuries and is left concentrating on a skull by the light of a guttering candle. The Louvre *Magdalen* (Plate

26) produces the same mood by different means. The serenity of the night-light pervades the whole picture. There is the feeling that the Magdalen will sit there for ever in that airless space. She is depicted with the same obsessive melancholy that characterizes *The Flea Catcher*.

In his time, La Tour's preoccupation with the human condition was a great rarity south of the Netherlands. French painters from Vouet to Poussin concentrated on the decorative and intellectual content of their work and were very rarely moved, as La Tour was, to depict scenes realistically. In *Christ in the Carpenter's Shop* (Plate 30), La Tour was even bold enough to try to depict the emotions of a child, although he used highly artificial means to achieve his end. From half way down the Grande Galerie of the Louvre, *Christ in the Carpenter's Shop* appears to be a curiously stilted composition. Joseph's back is arched over the top of the picture in an awkward manner. But on closer inspection the picture emerges as a masterpiece, both technically and aesthetically. The lighting is carefully modulated to produce a flickering pattern of tiny highlights and broader half-tones. As the Christ Child helps his father struggling with his work, the light of the candle is shown – a miracle of technique – shining through the child's hand, even to the point of showing the dirty fingernails. La Tour was able to relate the figures to each other beautifully. Both Joseph and the Child appear to us today as convincing people who inhabited a real world and not as images created to satisfy the whims of religious or government propaganda.

The same child model appears in the other great picture of this type, *The Dream of St. Joseph* (Plate 31). The smaller size of this picture is probably caused by the fact that it has been cut at the right and may well have been cut at the bottom. This makes the composition a little uneasy. La Tour lavished all his technical skill on certain parts of the picture, especially the child's profile and the wonderfully painted sash. The colour – ochre, vermilion red and a deep plum colour also found in the *Christ in the Carpenter's Shop* – is a little eccentric. But again the high point of the picture lies in the child's expression. La Tour has captured to perfection the moment of surprise as the wide-eyed and innocent child appears before the old man who has dozed off while reading his book. And, as in some of his other pictures, La Tour displays an originality of subject matter: there seem to be few other instances of Joseph being depicted with a book.

The picture of the type of *The Dream of St. Joseph* are very private and personal. It is not known for whom they were painted or what the type of person appreciated them. Some writers have assumed that they went straight into local convents, others suggest the houses of the local bourgeoisie as more likely resting places. Whatever the case, these pictures are very different from those compositions that are usually associated with *known* patrons and which therefore represent the public aspect of La Tour's art. They are far less intimate, they contain more figures.

With these public pictures, history has been particularly unkind. Although the surviving documents are quite explicit and appear complete, it is with the greatest difficulty that the surviving pictures can be attached to them. Even when the subject matter clearly corresponds with that of the documents, as with *St. Alexis,* the picture itself is hardly good enough to be from La Tour's hand.

The most important public subject – indeed the most important subject in the whole of La Tour's art – is that of St. Sebastian. One picture of this subject is certainly documented – it was paid for by the town of Lunéville in 1649 – and two other compositions, already referred to, were mentioned by Dom Calmet. Two quite distinct compositions of *St.*

Sebastian survive from La Tour's hand. The first, horizontal in format, exists in at least nine versions, the best of which is reproduced here (Plate 34). The other composition, in two versions (Plates 42 and 43), is upright.

Clearly St. Sebastian was La Tour's most popular motif. The horizontal composition has a dramatic intensity. The use of the candlelight is unusually ambitious as it involves so many figures illuminated by the candle flickering through the open door of the lantern. It is typical of La Tour to choose a moment of utter calm after the gruesome scene of near-martyrdom (in tending his wounds, the Holy Irene finds that Sebastian is not in fact dead and nurses him back to health.) There is no means of knowing whether this composition was the one referred to by Dom Calmet, but on grounds of style it is unlikely to date from the very last years of La Tour's career after 1645.

A *Nativity* was paid for by the town of Lunéville in 1644 and this has usually been considered to be the picture which has been in the Louvre since 1926 (Plate 36). This assumption is based on a similarity with the signed and dated *Penitent St. Peter* of 1645 (Plates 38 and 39). The picture was obviously an important composition. It is virtually lifesize and has a large number of figures. Today it is much damaged and has lost some of its crispness, but it remains as a touching depiction of the Bible story with an especially endearing Christ Child and down-to-earth shepherds.

It is not known how many of La Tour's major compositions are lost, but several are known from very inferior copies or engravings. Three of these survive. One depicts a composition similar to, but not identical with, the Le Mans *Ecstasy of St. Francis*; the second is a half-length composition very close to the upper half of the Washington *Magdalen*; and the third is a St. Anne and the Virgin keeping their vigil over the sleeping Christ Child (Plate 35). By some accident of history, a piece of this composition has survived, cut from what must have been a very large picture and therefore understandably in a damaged state. It was always thought to represent the Virgin and Child, but recent removal of overpaint has revealed a small piece of the Virgin's red robe; it is St. Anne who appears in the surviving fragment – a sad reminder of the incompleteness of our knowledge of La Tour's work.

The survival of the *Penitent St. Peter*, signed and dated 1645, should, by logic, serve as the cornerstone for the reconstruction of the last phase of La Tour's career. But in fact it offers very few clues to his stylistic development. It is utterly different from the other signed and dated picture, the Nantes *Denial of Peter* of 1650, and not strikingly close to other pictures certainly by La Tour (with the possible exception of the Louvre *Adoration of the Shepherds*.)

When viewed, the picture tends to be a disappointment; its colour is subdued and its tone quite dark. The lightest area is the lantern at the Saint's feet. But, since the composition is life-size, the most moving part of the picture – the stream of tears running down the saint's face – is rather difficult to see. The slate-greys and bottle-greens give the whole a leaden quality in perfect harmony with the picture's mood. The cock that reminds Peter of his denial stands out, strident against the shadowy background.

Nobody is quite sure when La Tour painted one his very best pictures, the *Newborn Child* (Plates 40 and 41). It does not fit easily into the pattern of pictures so far discussed, for its technique is rather different. It has been in the Rennes museum since the end of the eighteenth century. For over a century, it was attributed to the brothers Le Nain. It has been acknowledged as a La Tour since Voss's article of 1915, although there is nothing similar surviving from his hand.

The picture is unique. The model for the Virgin bears some resemblance to the Holy Irene in the horizontal *St. Sebastian*, although in that picture her face is much coarser. Even the tonal simplifications in the *Dream of St. Joseph* have been surpassed. In this one picture, and this alone, La Tour has entered another world. It is the hieratic world of the middle-ages, of Gothic sculpture, of the superstitious image, except that the paraphernalia of religion for the illiterate has been removed. The Virgin appears almost Buddha-like as she watches over the Christ Child wrapped in the swaddling cloth. St. Anne keeps her vigil, her lilac dress with its bottle-green sash making an acid contrast to the almost pure vermilion of the Virgin's robe. La Tour has become totally inscrutable. From a visual point of view, the picture is calm and balanced, its colour unique in the whole of seventeenth-century art. From an intellectual point of view, the picture refuses to reveal its meaning. The assumption that it is the Virgin and Child is reasonable, but no religious symbol is included. La Tour eschewed the clutter of his time, when every saint either waved or wore advertisements of his virtue or method of martyrdom. Instead he created a timeless Nativity.

By contrast, La Tour could also be downright sentimental in his attitude towards religion. St. Peter's tears arouse compassion. His *St. Alexis* also belongs to this category. St. Alexis was a local saint noted for his piety. La Tour depicted the moment when he was found dead underneath the stairs of the house where he had lived, a paper in his hand relating his life story. A picture of this subject was paid for by the town of Lunéville in 1649 and as the picture in the Musée Historique Lorrain at Nancy more or less corresponds to the artist's late style it may well be a good studio version of the lost original.

Problems of authenticity still bedevil any attempt to give a coherent account of La Tour's last years. Theoretically the job should be easy. It is clear from the documents that he was successful. La Tour painted in a very personal style of such high quality that inferior imitations are obvious. But the repetitions and replicas of his work, especially of his late compositions, present some severe problems. It is, for instance, relatively easy to arrange the nine versions of the horizontal *St. Sebastian* in order of quality; but it is very much more difficult to decide on the status of an obvious masterpiece like the Berlin *St. Sebastian*. Until a slightly better version turned up, this picture had always been regarded as the epitome of the painter's maturity. Its condition is unusually good and the condition of the better version (Plate 42) is unusually bad. It has all the characteristics reasonably associated with La Tour's later phase – chiselled features, dramatic contrasts of light, an air of hieratic calm.

The discovery of the better version just after the last war in a remote French church came as a shock to many scholars. The colour is very much more intense and the profiles more subtle. But how much of the Berlin version was due to La Tour? The documentary evidence is tantalizing. One of La Tour's many children, Etienne, born in 1621, became a painter under his father's direction. La Tour instructed that, should he die prematurely, Etienne should continue painting in the same style. The subsequent history of Etienne's career suggests that this did not happen. He moved to Vic-sur-Seille on his father's death in 1652 and back to Lunéville a few years later. He became a respected pillar of society and is no longer documented as a painter. Yet he did paint: what is probably his signature appears on a picture of modest quality in the Frick Collection, New York – an *Education of the Virgin*. Perhaps he painted the Berlin *St. Sebastian*, along with some other 'near miss' La Tours. There is simply not enough evidence to say.

As if this were not confusing enough, the last two pictures to survive from La Tour's hand – *The Denial of Peter* (Plate 46) and *The Dice Players* (Plate 47) – have been attacked by many critics, although both are signed and one is dated.

These large compositions are different again. Their abbreviated tones disconcert and even shock. The intimate and closed world of *The Dream of St. Joseph* has gone and has given way to a vulgar world of gambling soldiers in an eerie light. La Tour was no longer interested in distilling a perfect image of a simple child or a sleeping old man. Instead he chose complex compositions of unpleasant characters amusing themselves.

The Denial of Peter is an uneasy picture. Arms jut out awkwardly and the faces grimace in an un-La Tour-like way. Yet the picture is very likely to be *The Denial of Peter* paid for by the town of Lunéville in 1651 for presentation to La Ferté. It is not in good condition and has suffered much from insensitive restoration. Its colour scheme is a flickering harmony of reds and lilacs broken by large areas of dense shadow.

The Dice Players is generally thought to be La Tour's last surviving picture. It is slightly weaker than *The Denial of Peter* in conception although it is in very much better condition. But even here where the poses are awkward to the point of caricature. La Tour has produced several memorable images – the satisfied air of the old man on the left smoking his pipe, staring unmoved at the three young soldiers gambling the night away. But the most beautiful image of all is the androgynous figure on the right wearing a large pearl ear drop with an expression worthy of the *Newborn Child*. Clearly, this is not a spectator of a low-life scene.

It is easy to see what makes La Tour so very special for present-day taste. He combined a down-to-earth, analytical approach with a lofty detachment. His pictures also have great impact. It comes as a surprise to be confronted with the scale of his works. Most of his pictures are life-size, which gives them a physical monumentality.

This in turn poses the question of how they could *all* have been ignored for so very long. There is, as yet, no answer, for the history of each picture is almost always confused or non-existent. What is known about *The Dice Players* may serve as an example. Recent research has found that it may have passed through Christie's in the 1840s, although this is by no means certain. The first real record of its existence came in 1930, when it was bequeathed by a certain Annie Elisabeth Clephan of Leicester to the then borough of Stockton-on-Tees, County Durham, as a memorial to her father, Edwin Clephan. He had been an amateur painter and a supporter of the Leicester Art College. The picture was listed in the 1934 typescript inventory made by the borough engineer as 'De La Tour – old painting'. It was exhibited for the first and only time for one week in August 1944 and was then returned to store where it was discovered in January 1972. While in private ownership it may have been appreciated, although no record of the Clephans' interests in their pictures has been found amongst their papers. But what is certain is the fact that from 1930 until 1972, when it was in public ownership, it was neglected, allowed to deteriorate, and utterly ignored by those responsible for its care.

A number of La Tour's pictures belonged to painters themselves. Apart from *The Dice Players*, this applies to the Stockholm *St. Jerome*, *Job Mocked by his Wife*, a profile version of the *Hurdy-Gurdy Player* at Remiremont and the Chrysler *St. Philip*. His pictures rarely formed part of great collections (the major exception being the relatively minor *St. Jerome Reading*, which has been in the British Royal Collection since 1660). His absence from such collections meant that on the whole La Tour's pictures were ignored by the major art critics – art criticism is, on the whole, a product of capital cities rather than the provinces. (Stendhal noted the '*ignoble et effroyable vérité*' of the Nantes *Hurdy-Gurdy Player*, but he was in fact merely repeating the words of another writer, Mérimée, and not relying on a personal experience of the picture itself.) The English speaking world has been even more reticent. No nineteenth-century novelist eulogized La Tour's spiritual simplicity (in contrast to the treatment accorded Botticelli).

Now that La Tour is considered an important painter, what of the future? Will La Tour return to oblivion, remaining only as an interesting example of late twentieth century taste in the old masters? Some critics believe that this will happen. The curators of some great picture galleries do not wish to see La Tour represented on their walls and one eminent critic has consistently avoided La Tour when discussing the flowering of painting in the seventeenth century. La Tour was put on the map by the 1972 exhibition. Few people have seen much of his work, unless they visited that exhibition. It is too early to say what will happen. It is, however, tempting to draw a parallel with Vermeer, who was launched in 1866 by a great critic, Thoré-Bürger, in an article in the *Gazette des Beaux-Arts*. La Tour had a less impressive launch; but if the reputation of La Tour lives on as the creator of a series of serene images of human dignity, the efforts of Joly, the Lunéville archivist, and those who came after him will not have been in vain.

Outline Biography

1593 Born the son of a baker at Vic-sur-Seille (Moselle) which was then under the jurisdiction of the bishop of Metz.

1617 Married Diane Le Nerf, daughter of a wealthy Lunéville family.

1620 Moved to Lunéville (Meurthe-et-Moselle) in the Duchy of Lorraine, where he set up a studio and started to take apprentices.

1621 Birth of the artist's son Etienne who was destined to become a painter in his father's style.

1623-4 The Duke of Lorraine bought two pictures from the artist, both for small sums; one was described as an 'Image St. Pierre'.

1639 The artist described himself as 'peintre ordinaire du roi' (Louis XIII of France) and this may have been the time when he painted a St. Sebastian for the king, although this can only be surmised from an eighteenth-century source.

1644 Painted a Nativity for the town of Lunéville which was intended as a present for the Maréchal de La Ferté, governor of the duchy.

1645 Painted the Penitent St. Peter.

1649 Painted a St. Alexis for presentation to La Ferté.

1650 Painted a St. Sebastian for presentation to La Ferté.

1651 A Denial of Peter was presented to La Ferté. This is probably the picture at Nantes, dated 1650.

1652 Died in Lunéville 'd'une pleuresie'.

Bibliography

Since La Tour is such a recent discovery, almost all the literature before the 1972 exhibition at the Orangerie, Paris, is of great interest in the history of art and criticism. It is, however, of little use to the general reader and almost all of it is in French. The best general summary, when only nine pictures were attributed to La Tour, is by Charles Sterling in the exhibition catalogue, Paris, Orangerie des Tuileries, *Les Peintres de la Réalité*, 1934. This was followed by the full scale and extensively documented *Georges de La Tour* by François-Georges Pariset, Paris, 1948. All the known information was collated and much new material introduced in the exhibition catalogue under the editorship of Jacques Thuillier and Pierre Rosenberg: Paris, Orangerie des Tuileries, *Georges de La Tour*, 1972. Since the exhibition several monographs have appeared in many different languages from Japanese to Hungarian. The only one in English is by Benedict Nicolson and Christopher Wright, *Georges de La Tour*, Phaidon, 1974.

List of Plates

15

1. *Peasant's Wife*. Detail of Plate 3.

2. *Peasant*. Probably painted before 1620. San Francisco, California Palace of the
Legion of Honor

3. *Peasant's Wife*. Probably painted before 1620. San Francisco, California Palace of the Legion
of Honor

4. *The Vegetable Eaters*. Probably painted *c.* 1620. Berlin-Dahlem, Staatliche Museen

5. *The Beggars' Brawl*. Probably painted in the 1620s. Malibu, California, J. Paul Getty Museum

6. *St. Judas Thaddeus*. Probably painted in the 1620s. Albi, Musée Toulouse-Lautrec

7. *St. James the Less*. Probably painted in the 1620s. Albi, Musée Toulouse-Lautrec

8. *A Hurdy-Gurdy Player with his Dog.* Probably painted in the 1620s. Bergues, Musée Municipal, Mont-de-Piété.

9. *A Hurdy-Gurdy Player*. Probably painted in the 1620s. Nantes, Musée des Beaux-Arts

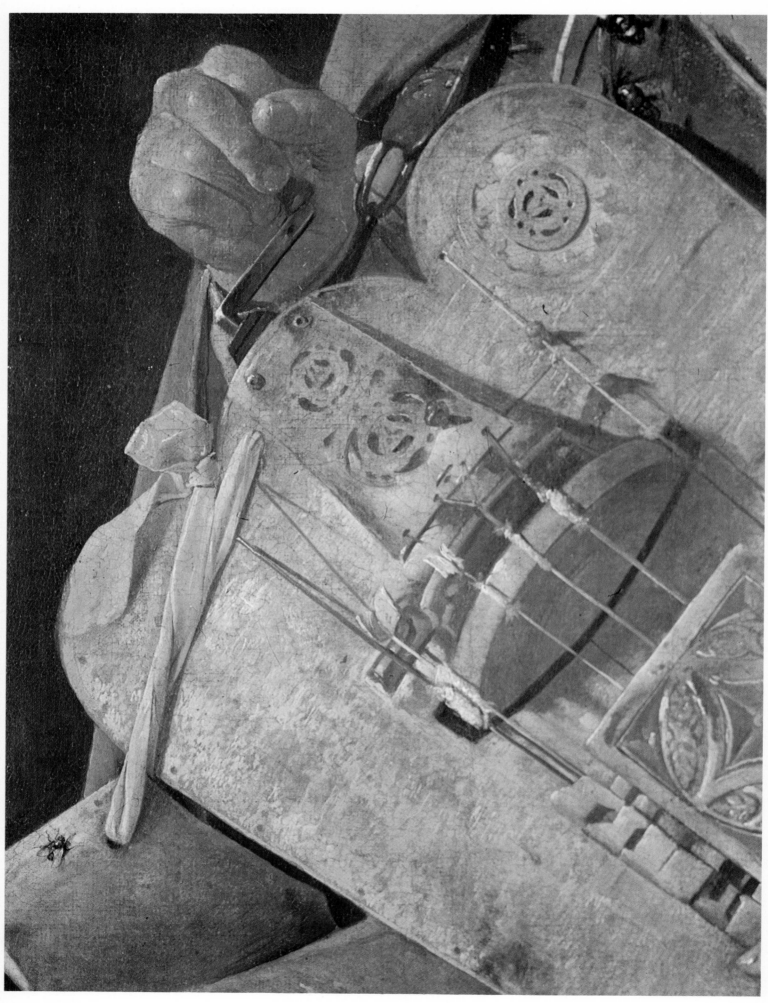

10. Detail of Plate 9

11. Detail of Plate 9

12. *St. Jerome*. Probably painted in the 1620s. Grenoble, Musée de Peinture et de Sculpture

13. *St. Jerome*. Probably painted in the 1620s. Stockholm, Nationalmuseum

14. *The Cheat with the Ace of Diamonds*. Probably painted in the late 1620s. Paris, Musée du Louvre

15. *The Fortune Teller*. Probably painted in the late 1620s. New York, Metropolitan Museum of Art

16. Detail of Plate 14

17. *The Cheat with the Ace of Clubs* (detail). Probably painted in the 1620s. Geneva, Marier Collection

18. *St. Philip*. Probably painted in the late 1620s. Norfolk, Virginia, Chrysler Museum

19. *St. Jerome Reading.* Probably painted in the late 1620s. Hampton Court Palace, Middlesex, The Royal Collection (Reproduced by gracious permission of Her Majesty The Queen)

20. *The Payment of Dues* (detail). Possibly dated 1641. Lvov, U.S.S.R., Museum

21. Detail of Plate 14

22. *The Flea Catcher*. Probably painted in the 1630s. Nancy, Musée Historique Lorrain

23. Detail of Plate 22

24. *Job Mocked by his Wife*. Probably painted in the 1630s. Epinal, Musée Départemental des Vosges

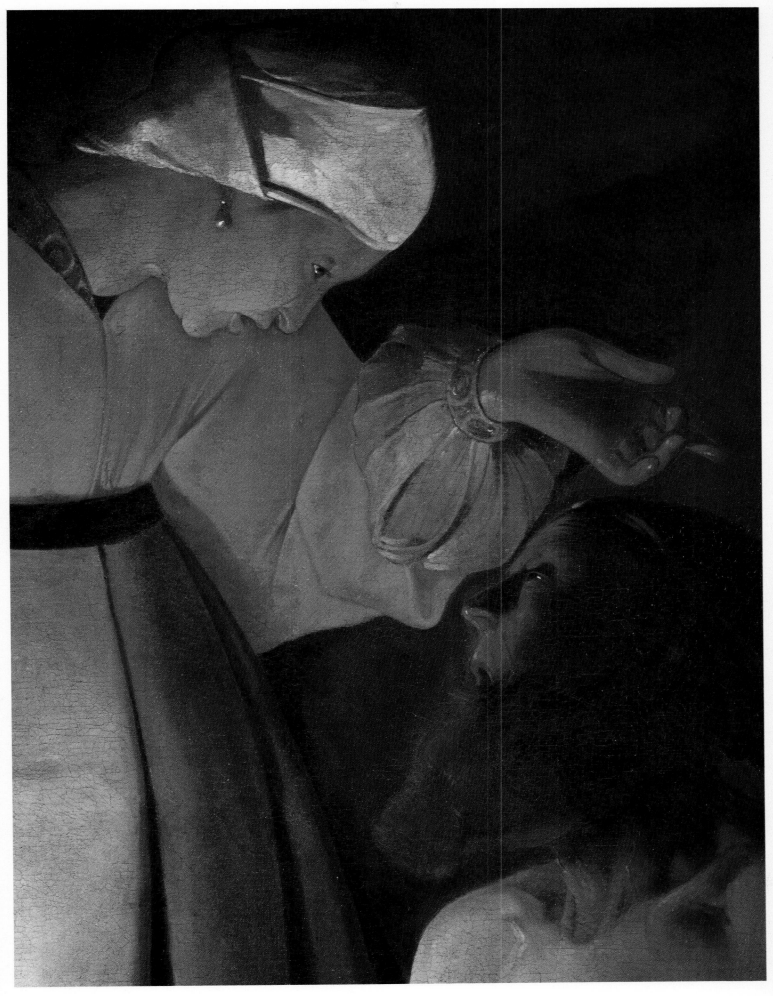

25. Detail of Plate 21

26. *The Penitent Magdalen with the Night-Light*. Probably painted in the 1630s. Paris, Musée du Louvre

27. Detail of Plate 26

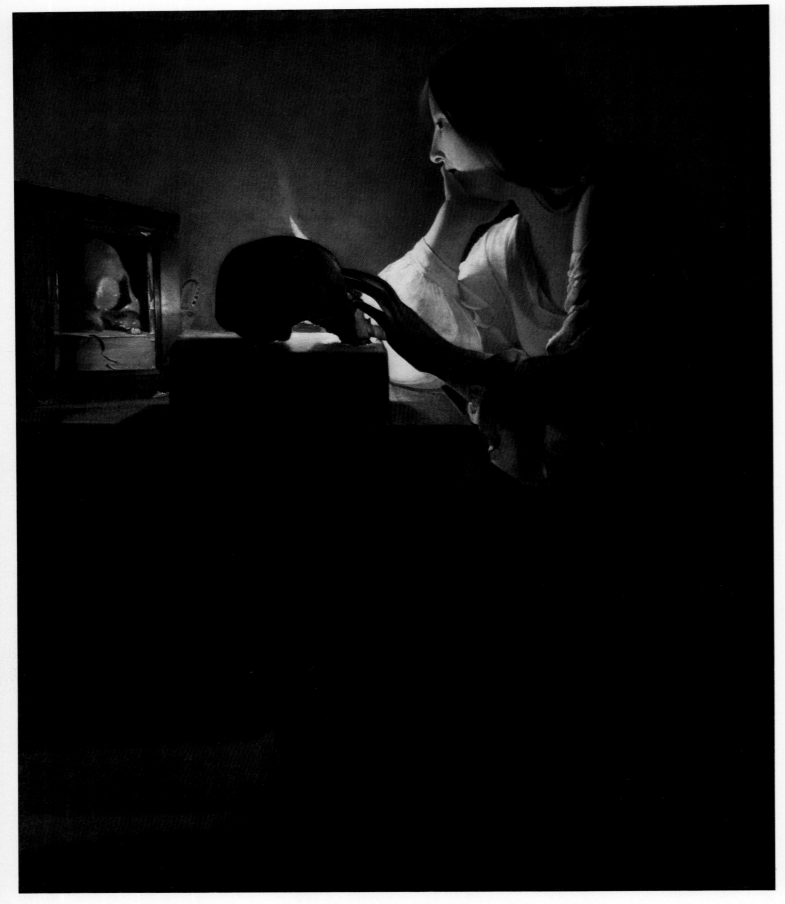

28. *The Penitent Magdalen*. Probably painted in the 1630s. Washington, National Gallery of Art

29. Detail of Plate 28

30.   *Christ with St. Joseph in the Carpenter's Shop*. Probably painted in the late 1630s. Paris, Musée du Louvre

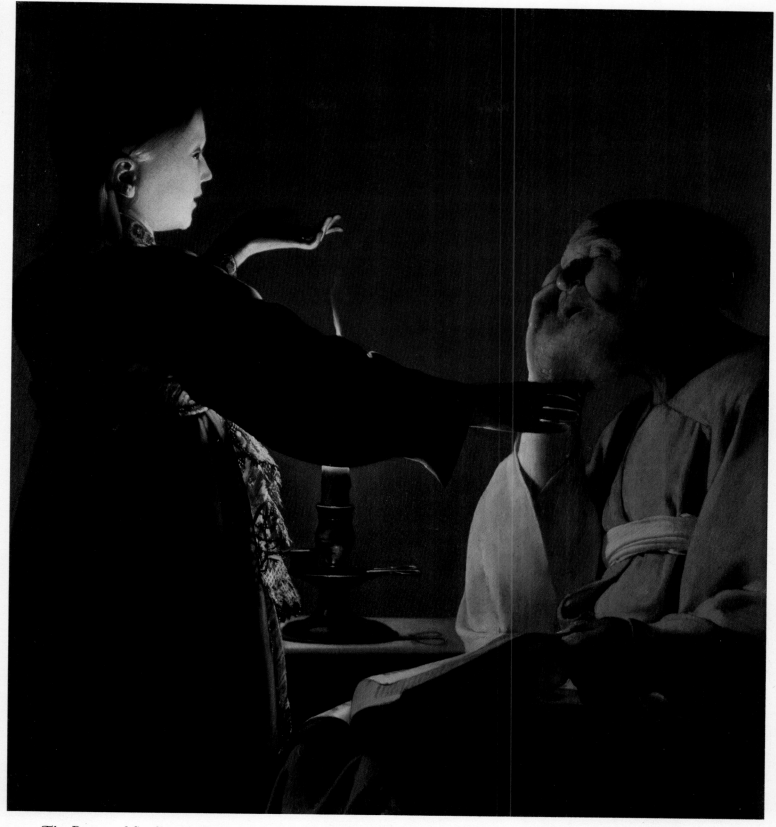

31. *The Dream of St. Joseph*. Probably painted about 1640. Nantes, Musée des Beaux-Arts

32. Detail of Plate 31

33. Detail of Plate 30

34. *St. Sebastian Tended by the Holy Women*. Probably painted immediately before 1640. Rome, Ottavio Poggi Collection

35. *St. Anne and the Christ Child (fragment of a Nativity)*. Probably painted in the early 1640s. Montreal, Private Collection

36. *The Adoration of the Shepherds*. Probably painted in or shortly before 1644. Paris, Musée du Louvre

37. Detail of Plate 36

38. *The Penitent St. Peter*. Dated 1645. Cleveland, Ohio, Museum of Art

39. Detail of Plate 38

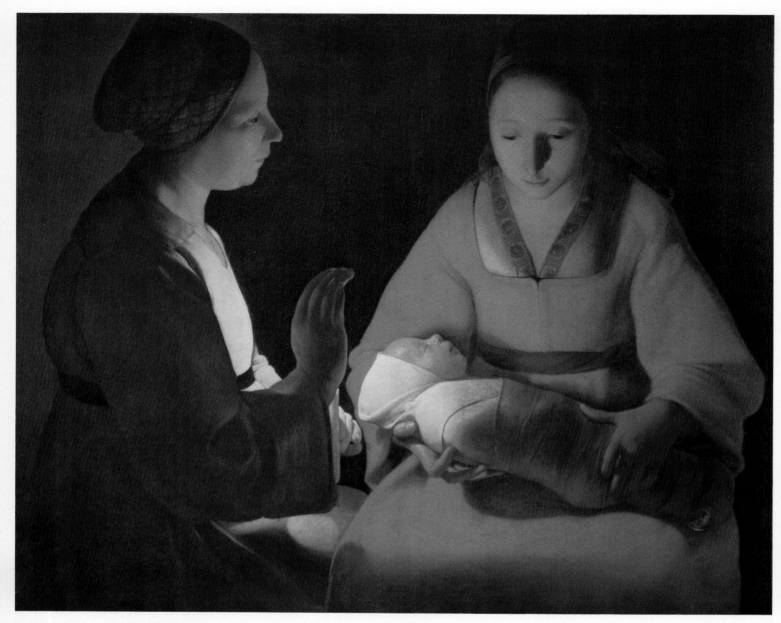

40. *The Newborn Child.* Probably painted in the later 1640s. Rennes, Musée des Beaux-Arts

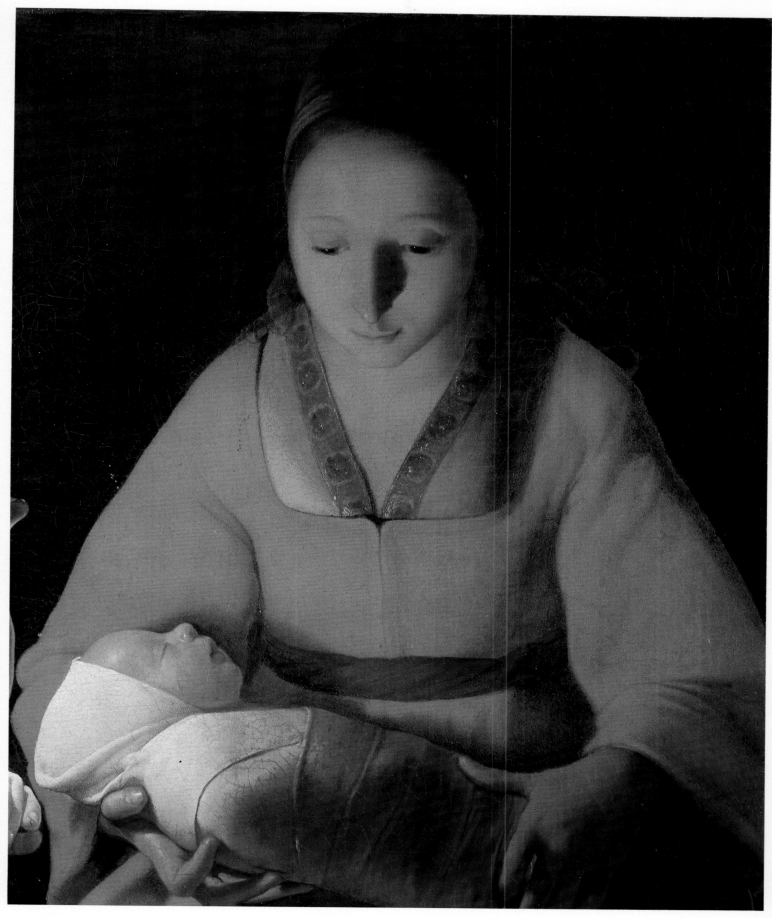

41. Detail of Plate 40

42. *St. Sebastian Tended by the Holy Women* (detail). Probably painted in or before 1649. Broglie (Eure),
Eglise Paroissiale

43. *St. Sebastian Tended by the Holy Women*. Probably painted in or before 1649. Berlin-Dahlem, Staatliche Museen

44. Detail of Plate 46

45. Detail of Plate 47

46.   *The Denial of Peter*. Dated 1650. Nantes, Musée des Beaux-Arts

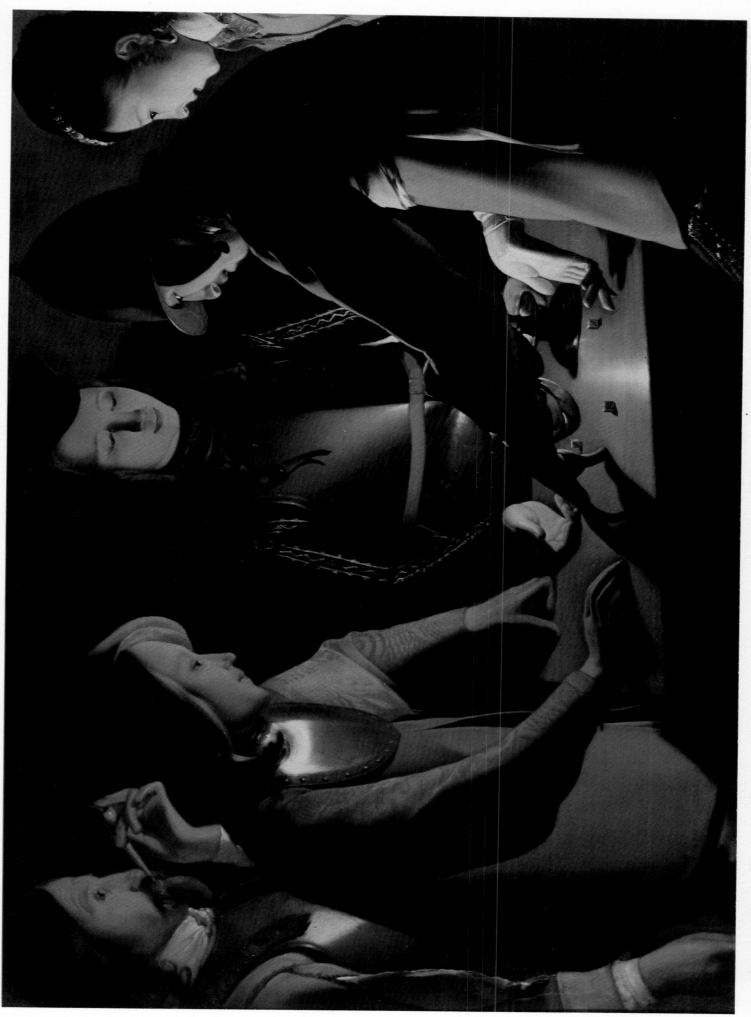

47. *The Dice-Players*. Probably painted about 1650. Stockton-on-Tees, Cleveland, Preston Manor Museum

48. Detail of Plate 47